T0160752

Ross's

Timely Discoveries

Michael Ross

Ross's

Timely Discoveries

Michael Ross

Rare Bird • Los Angeles, Calif.

THIS IS A GENUINE RARE BIRD BOOK

A Rare Bird Book | Rare Bird Books
453 South Spring Street, Suite 302
Los Angeles, CA 90013
rarebirdbooks.com

FIRST HARDCOVER EDITION

Set in Minion
Printed in the United States
Distributed in the US by Publishers Group West

Publisher's Cataloging-in-Publication data

Names: Ross, Michael, author.
Title: Ross's timely discoveries / Michael Ross.
Description: A Genuine Rare Bird Book | First Hardcover Edition | New York, NY;
Los Angeles, CA: Rare Bird Books, 2016.
Identifiers: ISBN 978-1-942600-83-1
Subjects: LCSH Books and reading—Quotations, maxims, etc. | Quotations, English.
|BISAC REFERENCE / Quotations
Classification: LCC PN165 .R67 2016 | DDC 808.88/2—dc23

*To my wife Ginny, our son Charlie,
and our daughter Margaret,
with deepest gratitude for all the
wonderful times we have shared*

Introduction

As I did in my first book of quotations (on men and women, romantic relations, love, sex, and marriage), I will offer some evidence of, or at least arguments for, my credibility regarding the topics in this volume. (Although reading *Ross's Novel Discoveries* prior to reading this one is recommended by the author, it is not required.) I hope readers will be satisfied, if not with my evidence and arguments, at least with my selection of quotations.

One qualification is my experience reading literary fiction. After surviving high school English class, and majoring in English in college (excelling in neither one), I became an avid reader. The academic experience must have had a salutary effect because I was exposed to numerous authors of classics, such as, Chaucer, Shakespeare, Dickens, Hardy, Tolstoy, Dostoevsky, Melville, Poe, and Twain. In addition, I was introduced to more modern authors, such as Faulkner, Joyce, Hemingway, and Fitzgerald. These experiences led me to more modern authors, such as Roth, Bellow, Wouk, Uris, Percy, Updike, Warren, and Salinger. From there it was on to even more contemporary authors, such as Auster, Doig, DeLillo, Pynchon, Gardner, Kennedy, Malamud, Powers, Russo, Irving, and Boyle. Lest one thinks that my reading has been almost exclusively US authors, I have read numerous works by British authors, such as Burgess, Orwell, Conrad, Maugham, Shaw, Huxley, Amis, Greene, and Fowles. Many other foreign authors have been part of my reading, such as some of my favorites: Nabokov, García Márquez, Kundera, Kazantzakis, Grass, Naipaul, Boll, and Davies. My reading has also included a number of female authors, including Eliot, Goudge, Dinesen, Welty, Porter, Cather, Rand, and Tyler.

I should confess here to two bad habits about my reading practices. I do not know how I developed the character flaw that led me to finish every book, at least every literary novel, I started. Perhaps it was an aversion to quitting, or an excessive optimism that the book would, regardless of the beginning or first hundred pages, get better. It has been only in recent years that I have developed the strength of character, or confidence in my judgment, to put down books unfinished if, after a fair trial, they lack something interesting to tell me.

My second weakness leads me to try to read as many of one author's books as I can after I have read one and liked it. I have been doing this despite my knowledge that the first, or first few books, by an author are often his or her best and later ones may not compare favorably to the earlier ones. One might say this about some of my early favorites, such as Barth, Heller, Vonnegut, Kesey, Pynchon, and DeLillo. There are, of course, exceptions, such as Davies, Hersey, Stegner, Gardner, Percy, Bellow,

Uris, and Greene, some of whose later books are, in my opinion, excellent. This idiosyncrasy explains why some authors are quoted relatively frequently in my books.

The other justification for my judgment about quotes on the topics in this book is the combined effect of my age, experience, and time for reflection, especially since retirement from my legal careers. The related topics in this book have long interested me. I have often wondered about the mysteries of time, especially our perceptions of both short and long periods of time, and how those perceptions change over time. There are often few answers to our questions, more often philosophic ideas and scientific theories. Past, present, and future may seem arbitrary and relatively easy to define, but they depend upon some sense of linear time, and their effects on us are often complex. Our age may affect our sense of the past, as there becomes more of it, our enjoyment of the present, and our perspective on and ability to contemplate the future, as there becomes less of it. Although I bristle at the notion of being labeled a "senior citizen" or included in the "older generation," I am losing, or have lost, my claim to middle age. I think it takes some mileage to select pithy quotes on youth, middle and old age, and memory.

As is the case with my first volume, readers will see that many of the quotes here could appear in a different section. There is natural overlap, and I did the best I could to make sensible decisions about where to put the quotes.

I believe in the value of quotes. They are used in our formal education and they crop up not only in literary fiction, but also in history, biography, and numerous other sorts of nonfiction. People recite them to us, we recite them to others, and we are guided, or, at least, informed or amused by them. Quotes may also introduce us to ideas and authors. Quotes can be instructive, interesting, and fun, sometimes all at the same time. We can enjoy them in solitude or share them with family and friends. I hope that readers will do both.

I will note in passing some of the quotes which have been especially meaningful to me. Readers are, of course, invited to find some quotes that stand out in some way for them.

Time and time again we wonder about time, perhaps more and more as "time goes by," which it seems irrevocably and irretrievably to do.

During my tours of duty in the Navy, I marveled at how slowly time passed for the men who were counting the days until their enlistment or term of service ended. My days, especially as Operations Officer aboard ship in the Mediterranean, sped by, as did the weeks and months as a young man visiting ports in Spain, France, Italy, Greece, and Turkey.

Practicing at a large law firm required me to log my time in fractions of an hour so it could be billed by the hour to clients. Nonetheless, days, weeks, and months passed quickly as I learned about corporate law and practice and became excited about the numerous big deals on which I was staffed.

Early life came in discrete numbers of years: three years of junior and senior high school, four of college and my service in the Navy, and three of law school. Then appeared the prospect of what we erroneously called a "permanent" job—more accurately a job for an indefinite time—for me at a law firm and later as an executive at a publicly traded company. The durations of these were determined by numerous factors, only some of which were within my control.

Time is of great interest not only to scientists and philosophers, but also to authors of, and characters in, literary fiction. They grapple with explanations and perceptions of time, making insightful and thought-provoking comments along the way.

Time is an appropriate starting place for this book because time is a fundamental part of each of the following topics: past, present, and future; age; and memory. It is time, of course, that creates our sense of past, present, and future, and in a chronological way establishes our age and affects our memories. Here are a few ideas about time itself, how we measure it, our perceptions of it, and its effects on us.

One of the recurring questions is if time, as we seem to know it, is only a concept we have created. To put it another way is to ask if time exists in some objective way, implying that our perceptions may be all there are:

«»

In English, there is an expression, "making good time," a colloquialism that if taken literally, implies that time is something that can be crafted or manufactured, and either poorly so or else expertly, a notion every bit as fanciful and illogical as naming a star "sitting trouser...—until one becomes acquainted with quantum physics, whereupon one learns that time, as measured by clocks on Earth, is, indeed, a contrivance, a thing we have conveniently made up.

Tom Robbins, *Half Asleep in Frog Pajamas*

Perhaps another good starting place would be to admit time's complexity, at least as we are capable of comprehending it. Here is a questioning reflection from one of my favorite authors:

«»

...I've learned that the primary law of Time and Space is that nothing is merely what it is.

John Gardner, *Jason and Medea*

Once we get to our perception of time, it makes sense to assess its value to us. A well-known author of classic children's books suggests in a novel for adults that time may be more valuable when we are not doing what society generally expects us to do:

《》

...and my time isn't valuable. What an idiotic expression. All time is valuable, and the time when you aren't working is much more valuable than the time when you are.

A. A. Milne, *Two People*

Although there are many admonitions about how valuable time is for us, here is an interesting way to describe why it is so valuable:

《》

"Everything," his father said, "comes down to time in the end—to the passing of time, to changing…. Anything that makes you happy or sad, isn't it all based on minutes going by? Isn't happiness expecting something time is going to bring you? Isn't sadness wishing time back again? Even big things—even mourning a death: aren't you really just wishing to have the time back when that person was alive? …Isn't it [commenting on photos] just that time for once is stopped that makes you wistful? If only you could turn it back again, you think. If only you could change this or that, undo what you have done, if only you could roll the minutes the other way, for once."

Anne Tyler,
Dinner at the Homesick Restaurant

Whether it is time itself or our perceptions of it, time does not seem to be consistent. Here is a thoughtful description, with a creative metaphor, of how it may differ from time to time:

«»

He had found that time itself changes in different periods of one's life—sometimes it seems fat with events and decisions, victories and defeats, each moment full—and in other periods time seems thin, one-dimensional, the hours long and slender, stretched like a wire.

Dan Wakefield, *Starting Over*

A recurring and key issue is how we measure time, because how we measure it may alter its effects on us. A very highly regarded highly regarded author's character has a strong view about how we often keep time:

«»

...he kept no calendar; his watch had stopped, he would not wind it up. It extended time not to hack it to bits and pieces. Perhaps this was closer to the Lord's duration. He was not much concerned with minutes, or hours, and after Creation, with days, except the Sabbath. His comfortable unit of existence was the universe enduring.

Bernard Malamud, God's Grace

Here are some more thoughts on the effects on us of measuring time with watches:

«»

In his thought men were much like their watches. The passage of time was marked as clearly upon a man's face as upon that of his watch and the marvelous mechanism of his body could be as cruelly disturbed by evil hazards.

Elizabeth Goudge, *The Dean's Watch*

The character in this novel comments on two very different perceptions of time, each of which we have all probably experienced:

《》

Now, once again, there were two kinds of time for him: the immeasurable and unnoticed time that passed while he was working, and formal time, the kind that is measured in seconds, minutes, and hours.

John O'Hara, *The Instrument*

When thinking back over time, or looking ahead, there are occasions when times and dates are prominent, or at least relevant, but there are other divisions of time that have been more important in my life:

«»

Just because we have invented clocks and calendars doesn't mean that's the way people keep track of their lives, do you think?

Jim Harrison, Sundog

Here is an interesting comparison of our ability to perceive of time and distance. How would the comparison work for days, months, or years versus distance?

《》

We are not really able to measure time because no gold second is kept in a case in Paris but, quite frankly, do you not imagine a length of several hours more exactly than a length of several miles?

Vladimir Nabokov, *Bend Sinister*

This one is puzzling. Could the question be whether there should be a time after which time would not be relevant? I confess that my legal experience does not help me with this one:

«»

Doesn't time know any statute of limitations…?

Ivan Doig,
Ride with Me, Mariah Montana

Another recurring source of contemplation is the speed of time, or our perception of time's different speeds. Another favorite author considers if the sense of time's passing slowly is an illusion:

《》

Just because things happen slow doesn't mean you'll be ready for them. If they happened fast, you'd be alert for all kinds of suddenness, aware that speed was trump. "Slow" works on an altogether different principle, on the deceptive impression that there's plenty of time to prepare, which conceals the central fact, that no matter how slow things go, you'll always be slower.

Richard Russo, *Empire Falls*

It seems the issue is not so simple as at certain times time goes by fast and at others it goes by slowly. Maybe, it can seem fast and slow at the same time:

«»

How quick and rushing life can sometimes seem, when at the same time it's so slow and sweet and everlasting.

Graham Swift, Tomorrow

Does the apparent change of time's speed, or some other characteristic, deceive us? A popular American author weighs in with a perceptive notion:

«»

Time tricks us into thinking we're part of her and then leaves us behind.

Jim Harrison, The English Major

Is time unfair to us as it changes speeds or appears to do so? This quote and the previous one assume time has a position of control over our lives:

«‹›»

But the cruelest trick of time was how it rushed you by the good parts.

John Casey, Compass Rose

The apparent increase in the speed of time can cause us more than a little discomfort, especially as we look back. Here is another focus on our control of time or lack thereof:

«»

It is the sweep of this life that gives vertigo, a sense of relentless departure. The rearrival on the coming tide is much more gradual and ordered, a processional, much like the paradigm of our own early years, which appear so painfully slow when we live them. No one is ready, it seems, for the loss of control, the ineluctable character of acceleration that gathers around later years.

Jim Harrison, Sundog

Our efforts to adjust to our perceptions of time may backfire, causing us to lose rather than gain time. It may be no surprise that this author offers thought- provoking irony:

«»

Moreover, the "better" time we make, which is to say, the faster we go, the less time there is, so that "by the time" we reach the speed of light, there is no time at all, indicating, perhaps, that the only good time is dead time.

Tom Robbins,
Half Asleep in Frog Pajamas

It is not only our own perceptions but also other's perceptions that change over time:

«»

"It is very strange how reputation will ignore the larger part of a man's life, choosing some particular event as an emblem for all of it. When you have lived as long as I have, you shall see how time turns great men into fools and vice versa. How men who were highly honored are now recalled, if at all, with a raucous fanfare of the black trumpet of Ill Fame."

George Garrett, *The Succession*

This author gives us a very concise and thoughtful description of time's effects on us and an admonition about what to do about it:

«»

Time takes things away from us if we don't fight to keep them.

Martin Davies, *The Conjurer's Bird*

Reflecting back on her life, this character makes an astute observation about a potential effect of time's passing:

《》

"The names of the entities that have the power to constrain us change with time. Convention and authority are replaced by infirmity."

Cormac McCarthy, *All the Pretty Horses*

The elderly character in this excellent novel offers very thoughtful and concise advice to a younger person about the sense of time's passing quickly. Perhaps, this is a good one on which to conclude this section:

«»

"Time passes you know. You will be surprised how the days slip along. Human life, even the longest is not very long."

Elizabeth Goudge, The Dean's Watch

For lack of a more creative idea, we will tackle these three concepts chronologically. So, the past will go first, followed quickly by the present, and then the unreachable future.

Throughout scientific and philosophic literature there are explorations of our sense of past, present, and future. In literature, narrators and characters reminisce with both positive and negative feelings, some of which may be skewed one way or the other by their biases and personalities. All agree there is no way to change the past, except, perhaps, by how we recall it. To make matters worse, some of what we think we remember is inaccurate, distorted by our regrets, successes, sentiments, and unmet wishes. Some suggest we cannot escape our past; others want to face up to, and make peace with, the past. There is also much speculation about paths not taken and their possible effects on our lives. There is no altering the past, and there is, without clairvoyance, no knowing the future. We can have hopes and fears about the future, and those will affect our present. And in between, how little attention we pay to the present. It is so fleeting, so difficult to capture, in a sense.

My past has been differentiated, perhaps like the lives of many readers, by academic years, professional occupations, and personal relationships. There were periods defined by my family, school, athletic, and social experiences in junior and senior high. There followed phases in my academic, athletic, and social experiences in college. Life as a naval officer, traveling as far west as Bangkok and as far east as Istanbul, created periods of my past according to my billets and deployments. My years at a West Coast-based, large, growing, and successful law firm, and later as General Counsel of a large, publicly traded company, defined other discrete blocks of my past. My sixteen years teaching practical seminars at two US law schools, one in China, another in Spain, and at a private university in Croatia, formed other segments.

My present is so fleeting that by the time I write about it, much less have this book published, it will have become my past. So too, the future changes with each moment of each day.

So how do we feel about the past? Here is a metaphor that reflects one perspective on it:

《》

Aren't we all sitting on stacks of past events? And not every level is neatly finished off, right? Sometimes a lower level bleeds into an upper level. Isn't that so?

Anne Tyler, Morgan's Passing

Sometimes the past seems remote or vague, a blur or gone altogether, but maybe it is with us in some way nonetheless:

«»

Even when it stands vacant the past is never empty.

Ivan Doig, The Whistling Season

One might well ask, as this character does, about when we obtain a past, in this case, one that may bode ill for the future:

《》

"But you may have a past, already? The darkest ones come early."

Willa Cather, *My Mortal Enemy*

Although many of us would like to redo or undo pieces of the past, here is a suggestion, with a creative metaphor, from a favorite of my younger days of a problem that would create:

《》

It would be convenient if one could redesign the past, change a few things here and there, like certain acts of outrageous stupidity, but if one could do that, the past would always be in motion. It would never settle down finally to days of solid marble.

Richard Brautigan,
An Unfortunate Woman

Some parts of our past follow us into the present. Whether it is this part, teenage years, or some other era, is open to debate:

«»

Our childhoods aren't so easily discarded, it seems.

Graham Swift, Tomorrow

Here is a memorable metaphor for the futility of trying to change the past:

«»

...not fearing the worst possible or probable because he owned the Cheyenne sense of fatality that what had happened had already happened. You couldn't change it and trying to was like throwing stones at the moon.

Jim Harrison, "Legends of the Fall" in *Legends of the Fall*

Here are some deep thoughts about the truth or falsity of our memory of the past:

«»

...and that wherever they might be they always remember that the past was a lie, that memory has no return, that every spring gone by could never be recovered, and that the wildest and most tenacious love was an ephemeral truth in the end.

Gabriel García Márquez,
One Hundred Years of Solitude

This creative author wants to disabuse us of the rosiness of the past, the false sense of how it was better than the present (those halcyon days), and he does it without pulling any punches. This is one that has stuck with me since I read it decades ago:

《》

Sentimentalists dream about the simplicity of the past, but the truth of the past is a truth of stupidity and coarseness and brutality and inconvenience, and of human beings stuck in the present like flies on fly paper.

Colin Wilson, The Philosopher's Stone

This author's narrator (the thinly dis-
guised author) has a profound doubt about
the past, that is, if it exists:

《》

*I sometimes wonder if there is such a thing
as the past. Perhaps it is all an illusion, a set
of false impressions dealing with possibilities
rather than actual things.*

Gore Vidal, Two Sisters

One often hears the adage that the failure to understand the past will condemn one to repeating it. This idea is quite similar but expresses the advantage of understanding the past:

《》

The road to redemption is to face up to the truth of the past.

Leon Uris, *Armageddon*

This question assumes that the past speaks or communicates, in some way, to us:

《》

...when you come right down to it, just where is the dividing line between reciting what the past wants you to and speaking gibberish?

Ivan Doig,
Ride with Me, Mariah Montana

Here is more about the past's effects on the present and future, and how we may or may not perceive them. A highly regarded Southern author delves, with a memorable metaphor, into the march of time:

«»

The mystery lies in the here and now. The mystery is: What is one to do with oneself? As you get older you begin to realize the trick time is playing, and that unless you do something about it, the passage of time is nothing but the encroachment of the horrible banality of the past on the pure future. The past devours the future like a tape recorder, converting pure possibility into banality. The present is the tape head, the mouth of time.

On a lighter note, the past may not, under the right circumstances, seem so bad after a while:

«»

Generally a reunion is an occasion with the worst of the past rinsed away by the passage of time,…

Ivan Doig, *The Bartender's Tale*

Whatever the past is or does, it may be disappearing before our eyes:

«»

We lose our past before we lose ourselves.

Gore Vidal, Two Sisters

One might quarrel with this suggestion about the clarity of the past, but I find the observations about the present very perceptive:

《》

"It's easy to look back at the past. It's not so easy to be clear-sighted about the present. We don't always know what we are doing now. We can just get dragged along."

V. S. Naipaul, *A Way in the World*

We may trouble ourselves trying to identify reality, a pretty heavy undertaking when it comes to our dealing with the past and present:

«»

...I am still asking myself which is the real life: the present with its discontent, or the retrospect with its emotion?

Thornton Wilder, The Woman of Andros

This one may not apply to everyone, or all the time, but there is a sense in which we are tempted to think things were or will be better than they are now. We can count on this prolific and very successful American author to put it very succinctly:

«»

Isn't it funny how paradise always lies in the past or the future, never exactly in the present?

John Updike, S

And if or when we get immersed in the dilemma, we might lose our bearings. The very prolific and astute British author puts it quite succinctly:

«»

Caught between the past and the future, he had no faith in either.

Anthony Burgess, *Nothing Like the Sun*

According to this notion, all three: past, present, and future, elude us. Again we find a well-put summary by another of my favorite authors:

《》

But the present is no less dark than the past, and its mystery is equal to anything the future might hold.

Paul Auster, "The Locked Room" in
The New York Trilogy

Yesterday, today, tomorrow; it can get pretty confusing if we are not careful. One of my favorite contemporary authors uses an enlightening metaphor:

«»

Tomorrow was just the light on the horizon, rushing to catch up with yesterday.

Richard Powers,
The Time of Our Singing

Here is a character's anxious concern about people who may figure in his future. Imagine if we could know who would be coming around the bend:

«»

Throughout life you meet people from the past, as natural as anything, but meeting someone from the future is far, far different. History only licenses us to drive in the past; the road ahead is always full of blind curves.

Ivan Doig, *The Bartender's Tale*

Without a proverbial crystal ball, the future is difficult to predict; yet the past may keep reminding of us its lessons:

«»

Odd that the future should be so difficult to bring into focus when the past, uninvited, offered itself up so easily for inspection.

Richard Russo, *That Old Cape Magic*

The character in this novel has a constructive framework for past, present, and future, one that I might find personally useful:

《》

To him, the past had once been the present... and the future. And if you looked at it like that, not only did it keep the past alive, it made the present more comprehensible and gave contour to the future's flat horizon.

William Martin, *Harvard Yard*

Even if we seem sometimes to know what is going to happen, it may not be a blessing. One of America's finest authors gives us pause to ask if we would want to know the future:

«»

Why did a man have to know ahead of time? Why wasn't the last knowing, when things finally came true, enough for a man to have to endure?

Robert Penn Warren,
Meet Me in the Green Glen

Here is another allusion to a trick time plays on us, this time applied to the future. This author was one of my favorites, and I was saddened by his accidental death that deprived us of more excellent novels:

《》

All the same, it was exceedingly odd, no denying it—the idea that Time was a trick of perception, like the solidity of tables and floors—the idea that the future was inevitable, had happened already and could no more be changed by human will, human love, than the fall of Constantinople. How sad and silly it made all human labor!—ten thousand lives wasted moving stones for a wall that was doomed to be overthrown in half a century, surgeons working hour after hour, bent like boxers, every nerve on edge, on the heart of a man who's been dead on the table from the beginning.

John Gardner, "Fragments" in *Stillness and Shadows*

In the proposed framework by this well-known British author, the message seems to be that our reliance upon a brighter future may dim our appreciation for the present:

《》

...the only faith of a majority of twentieth-century Europeans and Americans is faith in the Future—the bigger and better Future, which they know *that Progress is going to produce for them, like rabbits out of a hat. For the sake of what their faith tells them about a Future time, which their reason assures them to be completely unknowable, they are prepared to sacrifice their only tangible possession, the Present.*

Aldous Huxley, Time Must Have a Stop

Ah, the difficulty and inevitability of it all! But is it so difficult if we just let the future happen?

《》

The present was hard enough to deal with so that you couldn't very well handle the notion of the future. He had noticed that it arrived in daily increments without any effort.

Jim Harrison, "Westward Ho" in
The Beast God Forgot to Invent

Here is a very serious and rather pessimistic view of living for the future, because it may make us miss out on the present:

《》

You live in the radiant future, live for the future. You console yourself for the spectacle of things as they are by the thought of what they will be. And you work, perhaps, to make them be what you think they ought to be.... But a little reflection suffices to show how absurd these forward lookings, these labours for the sake of what is to be, really are. For, to begin with, we have no reason to suppose that there is going to a future at all, at any rate for human beings. In the second place we do not know whether the ideal of happiness towards which we are striving may not turn out either to be totally unrealizable or, if realizable, utterly repellent to humanity.... And finally, the contemplation of the future, the busy working for it, does not prevent the present from existing. It mere partially blinds us to the present.

Aldous Huxley, *Those Barren Leaves*

This is a very wise admonition about some dangers of too much time spent thinking about the possible problems the future may bring. Another of America's finest authors has Seneca give us a warning, one that I should take to heart:

《》

We all live too much in the future. Some things torment us before they should; others torment us more than they should; some torment us when they ought not torment us at all. We are in the habit of anticipating, or exaggerating, or imagining sorrow.

John Hersey, The Conspiracy

This is the longest section in the book. It is not simply because there are several parts to it; there were three parts to the preceding section. I submit that the reason is that authors and, of course, their characters feel strongly, and have more to say, about youth, adulthood, middle age, and old age.

It should come as no surprise that we will cover ages as they come to us. As time passes, we gain more past and lose more future. In the process, we age. It is difficult enough to draw lines between youth and adulthood, middle age and old age, as a physical matter, and it is all the more difficult with mental or emotional ages. Another dimension is that there are often some differences between how we perceive ourselves and how others perceive us during each age. And despite our generalizations, there come both plusses and minuses in each phase of life.

Readers may share my experience of giving little thought to my age until later in life. I may have considered the notion at milestones, such as, turning thirty, forty, fifty, sixty-five, and on special events, such as my engagement, wedding day, and the births of our son and daughter. Other events that triggered thoughts of my age include the passing of my mother and father and an uncle with whom I was very close. Avoiding too frequent consideration of age may be for the best because too great a focus on our physical age may not be healthy. I have decided it is best in small doses.

It seems best to start with a famous American author and a very positive metaphor for youth:

《》

Youth is like having a big plate of candy.

F. Scott Fitzgerald,
This Side of Paradise

A contemporary French author offers evidence of the evanescent character of youth, and a reminder of my own youth:

《》

If there was one thing that defined adolescence it was hysterical laughter. You never laughed like that again.

Antoine Laurain, *The Red Notebook*

In retrospect, at least, these exaltations of youth may seem a bit unrealistic, as this prolific and highly regarded author points out:

«◊»

...that greedy blind bliss of youth, when the world appears to be arranged by our impulses and full of convenient omens, of encouraging signs.

John Updike, *Roger's Version*

So, a recurring idea is that youth is the prime of life. Here is an author who is willing to pinpoint an age at which the benefits of youth are the most intense:

«»

Nineteen is the age of the perfect foot soldier who will die without a murmur, his heart aflame with patriotism. Nineteen is the age at which the brain of a nascent poet in his rented room soars the highest, suffering gladly the assault of what he thinks is the god in him. Nineteen is the last year that a young woman will marry purely for love.

Jim Harrison, "Revenge" in
Legends of the Fall

It seems appropriate to counterbalance the preceding positive perspectives with a negative one from an author of an earlier generation:

《》

"People are always talking about the joys of youth—but, oh, how youth can suffer."

Willa Cather, *My Mortal Enemy*

Here is a popular contemporary author's character who doubts the wisdom and judgment of, at least male, youth:

«»

Young men need to be kept away from guns, bombs, women, cars, hard alcohol and heavy machinery.

Dave Eggers,
*Your Fathers, Where Are They?
And the Prophets, Do They Live Forever?*

After these rather short comments, here is a longer and very thoughtful retrospective by one of my favorite authors on the confidence but lack of experience of youth:

«»

Odd, how our view of human destiny changes over the course of a lifetime. In youth we believe what the young believe, that life is all choice. We stand before a hundred doors, choose to enter one, where we're faced with a hundred more and then choose again. We choose not just what we'll do, but who we'll be. Perhaps the sound of all those doors swinging shut behind us each time we select this one or that one should trouble us, but it doesn't. Nor does the fact that the doors often are identical and even lead in some cases to the exact same place. Occasionally a door is locked, but no matter, since so many others remain available. The distinct possibility that choice itself may be an illusion is something we disregard, because we're curious to know what's behind that next door, the one we hope will lead us to the very heart of the mystery. Even in the face of mounting evidence to the contrary we remain confident that when we emerge, with all our choosing done, we'll have found not just our true destination but also its meaning. The young see life this way, front to back, their eyes to the telescope that anxiously scans the infinite sky and its myriad possibilities.

Richard Russo, Bridge of Sighs

Perhaps, the character who expresses these thoughts has figured out some of youth's limitations:

«»

He doesn't mind any of it very much, he's just tired of being young. There's so much wasted energy to it.

John Updike, Rabbit is Rich

A nineteenth-century French author, famous for several classics, points out a shortcoming of youth, using a very memorable metaphor:

《》

Youth cannot afford to look at itself in the mirror of conscience when it begins to bend from the straight and narrow, though people of mellower years have long since seen that reflection of themselves: the whole difference between the two stages of life lies here.

Honoré de Balzac, Pere Goriot

Here is an interesting, and perhaps debatable, claim about youth's egotism:

《》

The young search not for love but for someone they can talk to about themselves or, best of all to find that most marvelous of creatures who will, without fatigue or apparent boredom, analyze them by the hour.

Gore Vidal, *Two Sisters*

Most retrospective commentary about youth is very favorable, and many characters wish to return to their youth, but is there any way to stay young?

«»

"*The secret of keeping young is to read children's books. You read the books they write for little children and you'll keep young. Your read novels, philosophy, stuff like that and it makes you feel old.*"

John Cheever, Bullet Park

We assume that with age comes wisdom and judgment, but that assumption deserves at least a comical or cynical challenge:

«»

But my experience is that as soon as people are old enough to know better, they don't know anything at all.

Oscar Wilde, Lady Windemere's Fan

And how about a twelve-year-old's perspective on parents?

«»

"...That's grown-ups for you. By the time we ever figure them out,...we'll be them."

Ivan Doig, The Bartender's Tale

Here is another skeptic, this one questioning the ability of adults to deal with their past:

«»

Enduring what couldn't be cured, she supposed, was what people meant by being adult, though it was ironic that so few of them...had mastered the skill themselves.

Richard Russo, Bridge of Sighs

Whenever we would establish the onset of middle age, it seems that getting there is a major part of the battle. But is getting there half the fun?

《》

The achievement of middle age is itself an achievement.

Edward Abbey, "Gather at the River" in *The Serpents of Paradise*

Middle age may bring some understanding of our past, but that understanding may not be a happy one, albeit one many of us have experienced:

«»

One of the odd things about middle age, he concluded, was the strange decisions a man discovers he's made by not really making them, like allowing friends to drift away through simple neglect.

Richard Russo, *Empire Falls*

Here is a rather pessimistic generalization about middle-aged men by an author who has a wry sense of humor:

«»

A middle-aged guy should check himself out every day and assess the devastation.

Garrison Keillor, Wobegon Boy

Maybe it is called "middle age" because it is somewhere near the middle of the prior and next generation. The author uses an imaginative metaphor to describe the frustration of middle age:

«»

Picking up after the last generation was task enough; getting hold of the next seemed to him like trying to tweeze out slivers in the dark.

Ivan Doig, *Mountain Time*

So, not only is time proceeding apace, but our understanding, perceptions, and judgments are changing, and, therefore, causing some confusion. One of my oft-quoted authors uses a biblical metaphor to describe some confusion in middle age, then in another instance suggests there may be some surprises:

«»

In middle age you are carrying the world in a sense and yet it seems out of control more than ever, the self that you had as a boy all scattered and distributed like those pieces of bread in the miracle.

...

Middle age is a wonderful country, all the things you thought would never happen are happening.

John Updike, *Rabbit is Rich*

Here is the earlier quoted author again, somewhat later in life, with that business about nineteen!:

《》

He lived as a victim, albeit prosperous, of those dreams he built at age nineteen when all of us reach our zenith of idealistic nonsense.

Jim Harrison, "Revenge" in
Legends of the Fall

Speaking of nineteen, what about the perception by a girl that age of middle-aged women?

«»

After a childhood of hungering to be an adult, my hunger had passed.... These middle-aged women seemed very tired to me, as if hope had been wrung out of them and replaced with a deathly, walking sort of sleep.

Lorrie Moore, A Gate at the Stairs

This is a bit of a longer consideration, by a popular American author (a continuation of an earlier quote from the same book), of the effects of middle age, concluding on a somewhat dour note:

But at some point all that changes. Doubt, born of disappointment and repetition, replaces curiosity. In our weariness we begin to sense the truth, that more doors have closed behind than remain ahead, and for the first time we're tempted to swing the telescope around and peer at the world through the wrong end—though who can say it's wrong? How different things look then! Larger patterns emerge, individual decisions receding into insignificance. To see a life back to front, as everyone begins to do in middle age, is to strip it of its mystery and wrap it in inevitability, drama's enemy.

Richard Russo, Bridge of Sighs

This British author uses the opening and closing doors metaphor in a different, and perhaps more positive, way:

《》

Few people can reach even middle age without knowing there are doors they might have opened and could open still.

Doris Lessing, Love, Again

After canvassing some of the downsides of middle age, here is an assessment that suggests that despite all those, there can be peace with one's self:

«»

Everywhere I go these days I seem to find myself surrounded by younger and younger humans. If one keeps hanging about, as I do, then the temporal horizon expands, the pursuing generations extend toward infinity. But why should I care? Sagging into my late middle age, I have discovered one clear consolation for my stiffening back (I never could touch my toes anyway, and why should I want to?), my mildewed pancreas, my missing gall bladder, my panza de cerveza, my cranky and arthritic Anglo-Saxon attitudes. And the consolation is this—that I am content with my limitations.

Edward Abbey, "Gather at the River" in
The Serpents of Paradise

So, when does this somewhat indefinite middle age begin, and what are its effects?

«◇»

A man of fifty cannot remake his life.

V. S. Naipaul, *Magic Seeds*

This author has middle age start later, and the result, looking both forward and backward, is a less than happy one:

«»

…recognition that my life from the age of fifty-three on was a matter of caretaking, of supervising my body like some feeble-minded invalid kept alive by tubes and injections in a greedy nursing home, and that indeed it always had been such, that the flares of ambition and desire that had lit my way when I was younger and had given my life the drama of fiction or a symbol-laden dream had been chemical devices, illusions with which the flesh and its percolating brain had lured me along.

John Updike, Roger's Version

For this author, middle age is a year later. Although there are mixed metaphors here, they are both very effective:

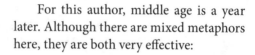

Well, by the time you're fifty-four, there's no eraser left on your pencil's end. You're condemned to those choices you made before you knew they were choices. All you can do is pay for the trip you've taken.

Elia Kazan, *The Understudy*

Leave it to this contemporary author to use a very dramatic metaphor to snap us into a sober sense of the middle age and the past:

«»

At fifty-five or fifty-six you still think you're a young man.... You still think you're going to live forever! And in fact you're attached to your youth only by a thread, not a cord, not a cable, and that thread can snap at any moment, and it will *snap soon in any case. And then where are you?*

Tom Wolfe, *A Man in Full*

Here is a somewhat humorous suggestion that being fifty-six years old may not be so bad if we resolve not to let it be bad:

«»

He was playing with the concept that there is no law that a man of fifty-six must stop all of living except sleeping and reading the newspapers and going to the bathroom.

Sinclair Lewis, *The Prodigal Parents*

This comment is about a bit of an older age and offers a physical inventory and a sense of occasional invisibility:

«»

They are both sixty-two now, and while neither of them is in bad health, neither of them fat or bald or ready for the glue factory, their heads have turned gray, their hairlines are receding, and they have reached that point in their lives when women under thirty, perhaps even forty, look right through them.

Paul Auster, *Sunset Park*

Here is a quote about getting chronologically older and exploring the feelings about aging;

《》

Sixty-five years old, he felt ageless, or ancient, which seemed almost the same thing.

William Kotzwinkle, *Hermes 3000*

One may well wonder about how to spend one's time as an older person:

《》

"At my age,…, there's so much time left over for thinking that a person can become a regular prophet."

Gabriel García Márquez,
"The Sea of Lost Time" in *Collected Stories*

With advancing age come some realizations about how your thinking has changed:

«»

You never think your own life is going to include the feeling "that was another age, another time, another world." But it does....

Graham Swift, Tomorrow

Here is another perception about how others, mostly younger people, view members of the older population:

«»

You live, she saw, surrounded by more and more strangers, to whom you are a disposable apparition cluttering the view.

John Updike, The Widows of Eastwick

This is a somewhat similar take on how older people might feel about their value to the younger generation:

《》

Thus Carol hit upon the tragedy of old age, which is not that it is less vigorous than youth, but that it is not needed by youth; that its love and prosy sageness, so important a few years ago, so gladly offered now, are rejected with laughter.

Sinclair Lewis, Main Street

Much of the contemplation of old age involves looking back at younger years and thinking about what they mean. It can become pessimistic or even downright cynical:

《》

This taboo regarding age is to make us believe that life is long and actually improves us, that we are wiser, better, more knowledgeable later on than early. It is a myth concocted to keep the young from learning what we really are and despising and murdering us. We keep them sweet-breathed, unequipped, suggesting to them that there is something more than regret and decrepitude up ahead.

Lorrie Moore, "Beautiful Grade," in *Birds of America*

This observation suggests that looking back may not be very helpful:

«»

It's usual to ask where the years went but I know very well where they went and sloppy sentimentality never did anyone any good.

Jim Harrison, "The Man Who Gave Up His Name" in *Legends of the Fall*

Although somewhat impolitely, this author seems to agree generally that the past has its issues, to say the least:

《》

...getting old is nothing but accumulating stupid shit we have to apologize for.

Richard Powers, The Echo Maker

There may, however, be a flipside, that is, a corresponding benefit in some effects of aging:

«»

The years bury so much of our wisdom that they are bound to bury most of our folly with it.

Eric Ambler, *A Coffin for Dimitrios*

Recollections in old age may be less about things done than about things undone:

«»

Nothing so much torments a geezer as the thought of the unlived life.

Jim Harrison, "The Beast God Forgot to Invent" in *The Beast God Forgot to Invent*

This author finds, at least, something positive in the reflections on the changes age brings to one who has reached old age:

«»

...It is strange how things turn and change. Strange the distance between beginnings and endings.... One of the few blessings of my old age is to have lived long enough to see how Fortune makes sport of our best hopes and wishes.

George Garrett, *The Succession*

Here is a very interesting and thoughtful notion about an attitude that may not change so much with age:

«»

There doesn't seem to be a big difference between having your whole life ahead of you and having only a small part of it left. The amount of hope seems the same.

Thomas McGuane, *The Cadence of Grass*

But, alas, there are differences that are not so pleasant, like this one:

《》

I've reached the age when sex isn't the problem so much as old age and death. I wake up with these in mind, and not a woman's body. I just don't want to be alone in my last decade.

Graham Greene, *The Quiet American*

Maybe there is still some mystery about being old, from the perspective of the old or the young;

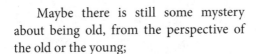

"Old age is very strange. It has a kind of aloofness. It's lost so much, that you can hardly look upon the old as quite human any more. But sometimes you have a feeling that they've acquired a sort of new sense that tells them things we can never know."

W. Somerset Maugham,
The Narrow Corner

It may be small consolation, but here is a proverbial silver lining that may provide some solace for being old. I found this idea obvious but one that had not occurred to me:

«»

She didn't know much about being an old lady—just think, every second you live, you have never been this old before....

John Updike, The Widows of Eastwick

The main character in this novel wonders if there may be a natural, attractive, and pleasing way to join the older generation:

«◊»

Growing old gracefully...the way has been signposted. One might say the instructions are in an invisible script which becomes slowly legible as life exposes it.

Doris Lessing, Love, Again

There will always be some who are unwilling to find much positive about aging:

«»

"Isn't old age loathsome?"…"Not sad, not dignified, not wise, but boring, tedious, stupid, shameful, despicable."

Elia Kazan, The Understudy

Well, one might as well make the best of it and look on the bright side. Some of us might find this idea tempting to use, at least, as an excuse for some behavior:

«»

...the capacity for being ornery was the one power left to a person in old age.

Ivan Doig, Bucking the Sun

Here is a perceptive observation about a difference between some elderly people:

«»

"I wasn't very wise, but it seemed to me that the crankiest, sourest old people were those that had lost the power to love. Whereas the old ones that seemed to be enjoying life, in spite of aches and pains, were the ones that look at life as a big joke."

John O'Hara, The Instrument

This may be an odd observation about elderly women and men, but who knows…?

«◊»

It is the fate of a significant fraction of little old women to turn into little old men: little old men in knickers and camisoles. You don't so often see the process going the other way, but here was…, a little old bag in a suit and tie. A little old boiler in gartered socks and black brogues.

Martin Amis, House of Meetings

This characterization may be a little harsh, but the notion of a two-way street is worth keeping in mind:

«»

Old age can often look like moral infirmity, and in real life to see someone suddenly old is like seeing a moral infirmity made suddenly clear. And then you understand that the other man is looking at you in the same way.

V. S. Naipaul, *Magic Seeds*

This seems at first to be a notion of how to accept old age, but there is an acute sense of irony about the relatively short duration of our youth:

《》

Her age does not surprise her. She's grown used to it by now. You're old for so much longer than you're young, she thinks. Really it hardly seems fair.

Anne Tyler,
Dinner at the Homesick Restaurant

But fair or not, obsession with the end cannot help, as this character puts it so well in his dialect:

«»

I calculate the main reason an old pelter like me has run on so long is that I'm not scared of dyin,' not a bit. Bein' afraid of dyin' is the most killin' pastime there is.

John Hersey, *The Marmot Drive*

Here is a series of very short, pithy commentaries on being old, beginning with one about the physical effects:

《》

Beauty. It's what you're left with when your joints give out.

Ethan Canin, America America

Here is a bit of a metaphysical metaphor
and, maybe, a "how to" prescription:

«»

But old age is some other kind of territory,
people exist in it by their own lights.

Ivan Doig, *Bucking the Sun*

This one is more serious and put quite thoughtfully. I wonder if I am telling more stories than I did when I was younger. If so, it may be because I have more to tell than I did then:

《》

You get old and you realize there are no answers, just stories.

Garrison Keillor, Pontoon

Here is a common realization that as we get older we see in ourselves more of our parents, for better or worse. I, for one, am guilty as charged:

《〉

"Yes, and because as we grow old we become more and more the stuff our forbears put in us."

Willa Cather, My Mortal Enemy

These last two are my favorites, the first by a favorite contemporary author:

《》

One reaches the age when being realistic isn't practical anymore.

Richard Powers,
Operation Wandering Soul

You have to admire the humor and irony of this one!

«»

Old age takes all the fun out of trouble.

Edward Abbey, *Good News*

Memory is a favorite topic not only for neuroscientists and psychologists, but also for authors of literary fiction. It is a critical part of our perception of our past and, therefore, our fleeting present, and it affects our perception of the future. One theme is how our memory works well or not so well to remember our past. It appears that forgetting is an important part of memory. That may sound odd, but imagine if our brains were wired to remember everything! It is always interesting to learn how people with whom we have shared an experience remember it so differently, as if there were two different events or situations. Memory, apparently, also plays a role in our perception of time's passage. Our memories come back to us, wanted or not, and can have meaningful effects on our mental well-being and our visualization of future events.

As I get older, I am more conscious of my purposeful exercise of both my short- and long-term memory, sometimes without a struggle, at other times with more effort and a need to put aside the effort and let the sought-after name or place come back to me by itself. I am also more aware of unintended flashbacks, triggered Proust-like, and as often as not, of trivial occurrences. It has been enlightening to compare memories with friends from the past to see how, if at all, they jibe. I find more and more frequently that my wife remembers things I did not say or do. Is this, perhaps, an example of extrasensory perception?

Perhaps, we should start by asking why we evolved with memories. Here is an answer with a memorable metaphor:

«»

But memory, always there in its bone house. What can it be for, remembering? To keep us from falling into the same ditch everyday, certainly. But more, too. Memory we hold up and gaze into as proof of ourselves. Like thumbprint on a window, remembering is mindprint....

Ivan Doig, *The Sea Runners*

This author offers an idea about how we might improve our memories:

«»

...that for memory to function well, it needs constant practice: if recollections are not evoked again and again in conversations with friends, they go.

Milan Kundera, *Ignorance*

Memory serves us well in both recalling and forgetting:

《》

...the memory of pain, even the most painful disappointment, finally vanishes. But memory of pleasure, and even of the hope that humbly attended it, is always near enough to be called forth like a benign, obedient spirit. For as long as memory will last.

George Garrett, *The Succession*

Here is a bit of a contrary view about which memories we keep and want to keep:

«»

I had still somehow to live and to remember memories in order somehow to eliminate them. Happy memories are the worst, and I tried to remember the unhappy.

Graham Greene, *The Quiet American*

Even if we could keep the memories we want and discard the rest, memory has a way of its own, as this prolific American author describes so well:

«»

Memory is fitful at best. People come and go at random in swift uncertain circuits of the brain, and with each year one loses more and more names and faces while even sexual encounters tend to blur one into another.

Gore Vidal, Two Sisters

One of my favorite authors focuses, perhaps with a bit of hyperbole, on the art of not remembering and its importance:

«»

The secret of survival is forgetting. If evolution favored conscience, everything with a backbone would have hanged itself from the ceiling fan eons ago, and invertebrates would once again be running the place.

Richard Powers,
Generosity: an Enhancement

Another author's character gives some advice along these lines to a young woman:

《》

"Much has been made of the doom of not remembering. But remembering has its limitations. Believe me, it is good to forget."

𝓛𝓸𝓻𝓻𝓲𝓮 𝓜𝓸𝓸𝓻𝓮, *A Gate at the Stairs*

Because he is a favorite author, here is another one from him—his sense in which memory performs double duty:

《》

I continually write my biography by my actions, mixing involvement with knowledge, accountable to those moments when both drop away to reveal the act of mixing—something a priori *recognizable. This process does not differ measurably from the way I come to understand others, my time or past times. Memory, then, is not only a backward retrieval of a vanished event, but also a posting forward, at the remembered instant, to all other future moments of corresponding circumstance.*

Richard Powers,
Three Farmers on Their Way to a Dance

This famous or infamous rogue journalist offers an interesting take on another way in which memory works:

«»

The scene I had just witnessed brought back a lot of memories—not of things I had done but of things I failed to do, wasted hours and frustrated moments and opportunities forever lost because time had eaten so much of my life and I would never get it back.

Hunter S. Thompson, The Rum Diary

And how might we react to remembering those roads not taken? I occasionally wonder about them, but not for long:

《》

Maybe a person simply cannot help getting the willies about what might have been.

Ivan Doig,
Ride with Me, Mariah Montana

But what if memory worked the other way? Here are some thoughts by the same author in an earlier novel:

《》

There are moments, central moments..., which form themselves unlike any that ever have issued in our lives or shall again. Ours might seem a kindlier evolution if what we know as memory had been set in us the other way: if these pith incidents of existence already waited on display there in the mind when you, I...come into the world—a glance, and scene A ready to happen some certain Thursday; beyond it, B in clear view, due on a Wednesday two years and seventeen days off. The snag, of course, is Z, the single exactitude we could never bear to know: death's date. In order then that we can stand existence, the apparatus fetches backward for us rather than ahead. Memory instead of foreknowledge.

Ivan Doig, The Sea Runners

A very distinguished writer of the American West shows us, with very descriptive metaphors, how memory can treat or mistreat us:

«»

Memory was a trap, a pit, a labyrinth. It tricked you into looking backward, and you saw yourself in another avatar, smaller and more narrow-visioned but richer in the life of the senses, and in that incarnation too you were looking back. You met yourself in your past, and the recognition was a strong quick shock, like a dive into cold water.

Wallace Stegner,
The Big Rock Candy Mountain

Does memory fool us by making our past picture-perfect? This answer uses a very recognizable metaphor:

«»

So much of what you think *you remember is a lie, the stuff of postcards.*

John Irving, *Until I Find You*

Here is an echo of the same sentiment, albeit a bit stronger condemnation:

«»

You often feel that you remember someone vividly and in detail, then you check the matter and it all turns out to be so inane, so meager, so shallow—a deceptive façade, a bogus enterprise on the part of your memory.

Vladimir Nabokov, "The Reunion" in *Details of a Sunset and Other Stories*

We tend to think most of our own memories and neglect to think how, if at all, others with whom we had experiences do or would recall them. I find this analysis very perceptive:

«»

I imagine the feelings of two people meeting again after many years. In the past they spent some time together, and therefore they think they are linked by the same experience, the same recollections. That's where the misunderstanding starts: they don't have the same recollections; each of them retains two or three small scenes from the past, but each has his own; their recollections are not similar; they don't intersect; and even in terms of quantity they are not comparable: one person remembers the other more than he is remembered; first because memory capacity varies among individuals (an explanation that each of them would at least find acceptable), but also (and this is more painful to admit) because they don't hold the same importance for each other.

Milan Kundera, Ignorance

One of Germany's most prominent post-war authors considers the role of memory for the elderly:

«»

Nothing but memory, scantily equipped. Nothing but an old man's lingering longing.

Gunter Grass, Too Far Afield

Memories may be very valuable at any age but, according to this author's character, a fictional character might have more capacity for living with memory than his real-world counterpart:

«»

His editor further argued that only in a book is a man willing to live forever with a memory.

Leon Uris, *The Angry Hills*

And for some people, memory can be too much of a good thing. Here is a metaphor readers may not forget:

«»

Dangerous to squeeze the tube of nostalgia. Never get the toothpaste back in.

Wallace Stegner, *Recapitulation*

An older person looking back may wonder about the relationship between the present and memories and, perhaps, become ensnared in a bit of a metaphysical quandary:

《》

If all you had out of living was the memories you couldn't remember the feelings of, did that mean that your living itself, even now while you lived it, was like that too, and everything you did, even in the instant of doing, was nothing more than the blank motions the shadow of your body made in those memories which now, without meaning, were all you had out of the living and working you had done before?

Robert Penn Warren,
Meet Me in the Green Glen

It seems only appropriate to conclude this section with a good quote that is easy to remember:

《》

Time didn't age you; memory did.

Richard Powers, *The Echo Maker*

Afterword

It may be trite to say that time is precious, but my daily life regularly consumes time unmercifully. After three or four (depending on how I count) occupations, and with our son and daughter away at college, I am giving a great deal more thought to how I spend my time. The work of collecting, organizing, and commenting on these quotes has been rewarding. Sharing these quotes with readers, who I hope will enjoy them, is very gratifying.

I am endeavoring, with varying degrees of success, to keep my past in its place, appreciate my present, and let my future come as it will, knowing what I can and cannot influence, much less control. One of my challenges is to be realistic about my physical age, without letting the number of years take on a disproportionate importance. Conscious and less-conscious memories affect my present enjoyment of life and my hopes and fears for my future.

I hope readers will have taken the time to discover some novel ideas about time; past, present, and future; age; and memory. These quotes will not have solved any mysteries about time, but they may have offered some constructive or instructive thoughts about our perception of time. They may, too, have suggested some interesting perspectives on the human condition of having a past, a so very brief present, and an indefinite future. Aging is something we take for granted through our youth and much of adulthood. We think little about aging and its consequences until, perhaps, middle age, and thereafter it becomes more and more relevant as we reach old age. I hope readers will remember some quotes, or if not, at least recall where to find them. Am I forgetting anything?

I would like to express my deep appreciation for Tyson Cornell's enthusiastic support and creative ideas for the second volume of my quotations, and for the hard work by all of the staff at Rare Bird, including Alice Marsh-Elmer for the development and execution of the excellent design, inside and out, of the book; Julia Callahan; and Winona Leon.

Thanks to Cara Lowe for the illustrations.